Theory Paper   Grade 3   2017   A
Model Answers

1

etc.

etc.

etc.

2   (10)

(a)

(b) six

3 E melodic minor   (10)

F harmonic minor

D major

A♭ major

4   (10)

5   (10)

6 C sharp   G / G natural   D flat   (10)

A flat   F sharp   B / B natural

7   (10)

8   (10)

prima volta means		**Presto** means:		*ritmico* means:	
first time	✔	slow		held back	
in time		fast	✔	agitated	
speed, time		at a medium speed		rhythmically	✔
second time		broadening		at choice	

non troppo means:		*semplice* means:		*rubato* means:	
very much		suddenly		at a comfortable speed	
too much		simple, plain	✔	with determination	
not too much	✔	in the same way		becoming more lively	
not in time		sustained		with some freedom of time	✔

9   (10)

(a) (i)   5th

(ii)   D major

(iii)   false

(iv)   7

(v)   dotted quaver / dotted eighth note

(b)   (10)

Theory Paper   Grade 3   2017   B
Model Answers

1 (10)

Alexander L'Estrange & Tom Pilling

2 (10)

(a)

(b) compound
    triple

3 (10)

4 major   major   perfect   (10)
    2nd   7th   octave / 8ve / 8th

         minor   perfect
         6th   5th

5 (10)

Valerie Capers

or

6 (10)

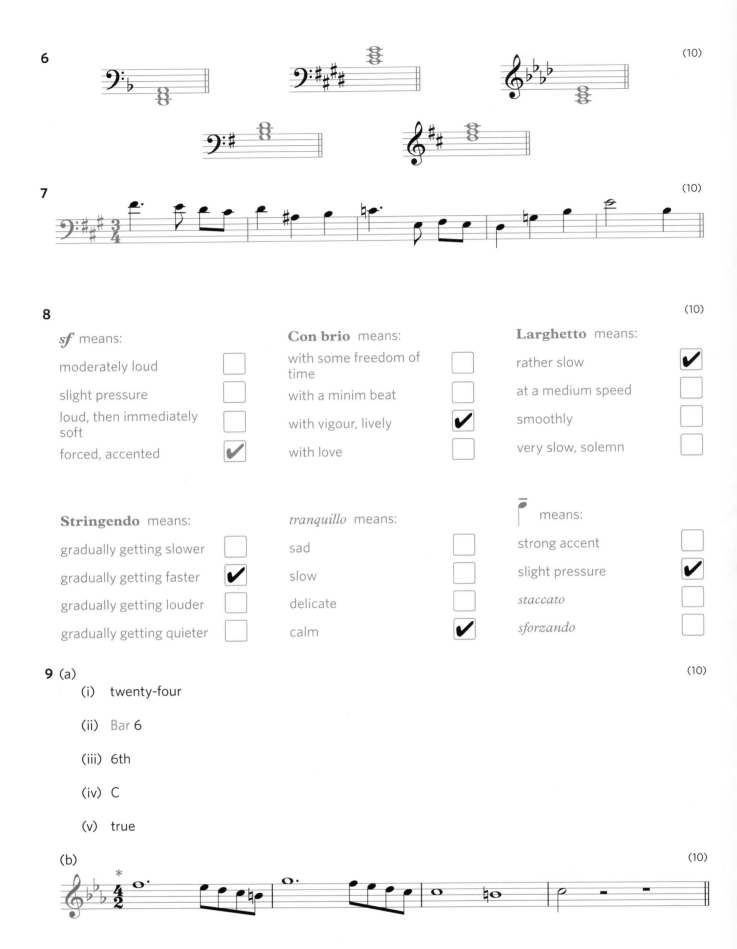

7 (10)

8 (10)

sf means:

moderately loud ☐

slight pressure ☐

loud, then immediately soft ☐

forced, accented ✔

Con brio means:

with some freedom of time ☐

with a minim beat ☐

with vigour, lively ✔

with love ☐

Larghetto means:

rather slow ✔

at a medium speed ☐

smoothly ☐

very slow, solemn ☐

Stringendo means:

gradually getting slower ☐

gradually getting faster ✔

gradually getting louder ☐

gradually getting quieter ☐

tranquillo means:

sad ☐

slow ☐

delicate ☐

calm ✔

͞‖ means:

strong accent ☐

slight pressure ✔

staccato ☐

sforzando ☐

9 (a) (10)

(i) twenty-four

(ii) Bar 6

(iii) 6th

(iv) C

(v) true

(b) (10)

Theory Paper   Grade 3   2017   C
Model Answers

1 (10)

2 (10)

Elissa Milne

'Groovy Movie' from *Easy Little Peppers* © 2004 Faber Music Ltd
Extract reproduced by permission of Faber Music Ltd. All rights reserved.

3 (10)

perfect	minor	major
4th	6th	2nd

perfect	major
octave / 8ve / 8th	7th

4 (10)

5 (10)

Ab major	F minor	E major

C# minor	D minor

6 (10)

F sharp	G flat	D / D natural

A / A natural	C sharp	E flat

7 (10)

♩. = 60 means:

60 dotted-crotchet beats in a minute	✔
60 dotted-crotchet beats	☐
60 dotted crotchets in the melody	☐
60 dotted-crotchet notes	☐

Allegro assai means:

fairly quick	☐
quick	☐
very quick	✔
gradually getting quicker	☐

più mosso means:

with movement	☐
more movement	✔
less movement	☐
without movement	☐

amoroso means:

agitated	☐
sad, sorrowful	☐
delicate	☐
loving	✔

risoluto means:

bold, strong	✔
rhythmically	☐
simple, plain	☐
becoming more lively	☐

scherzando means:

sweet	☐
simple, plain	☐
playful, joking	✔
forced, accented	☐

8 (10)

9 (a) (10)

(i) A minor

(ii) **Allegretto** ♩. = 60

(iii) six

(iv) dotted minim / dotted half note

(v) compound

duple

(b) (10)

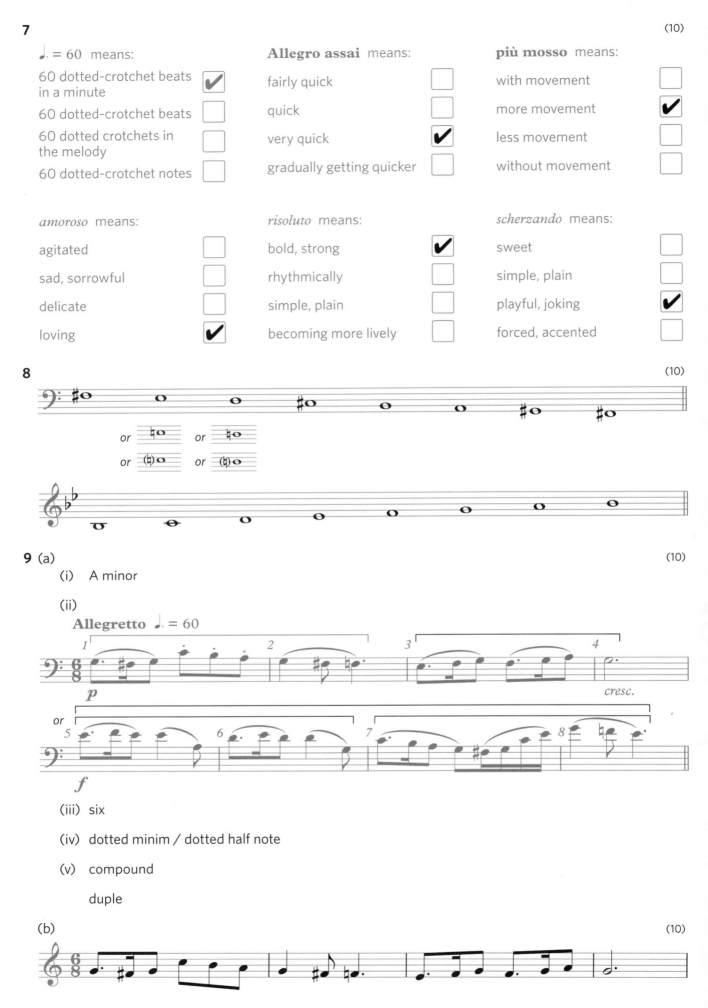

Theory Paper   Grade 3   2017   S
Model Answers

1  (10)

2 F sharp   D / D natural   C sharp   (10)

E flat   G flat   B / B natural

3 major   minor   perfect   (10)
3rd   3rd   octave / 8ve / 8th

major   major
2nd   7th

4 (10)

5 (10)

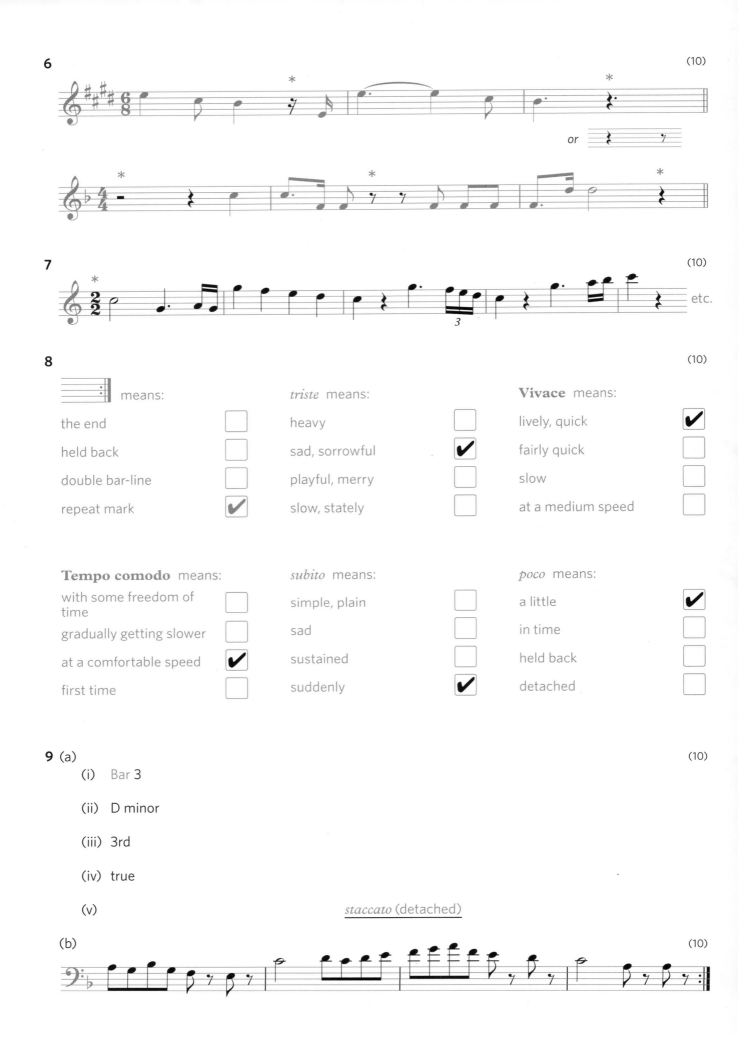

6 (10)

7 (10)

8 (10)

means:		*triste* means:		**Vivace** means:	
the end		heavy		lively, quick	✔
held back		sad, sorrowful	✔	fairly quick	
double bar-line		playful, merry		slow	
repeat mark	✔	slow, stately		at a medium speed	

Tempo comodo means:		*subito* means:		*poco* means:	
with some freedom of time		simple, plain		a little	✔
gradually getting slower		sad		in time	
at a comfortable speed	✔	sustained		held back	
first time		suddenly	✔	detached	

9 (a) (10)

    (i) Bar 3

    (ii) D minor

    (iii) 3rd

    (iv) true

    (v)   *staccato* (detached)

(b) (10)